Packing m

Annette Smith
Illustrated by Margaret Power

I put my sandwich
into my bag.

I put my apple  into my bag.

I put my drink into my bag.

I put my hat into my bag.

I put my book into my bag.

Hedgehog is Hungry

I put my picture into my bag.

I put my spider
into my bag …

... for my teacher!